Triumph
Over Tragedy

Triumph
Over Tragedy

My Journey of Healing
after My Daughter's Murder…

CHERYL ANN ROTTMAN

PALMETTO

P U B L I S H I N G

Charleston, SC

www.PalmettoPublishing.com

Copyright © 2024 by Cheryl Ann Rottman

Hardcover ISBN: 979-8-8229-4279-0
Paperback ISBN: 979-8-8229-4280-6
eBook ISBN: 979-8-8229-4281-3

DEDICATION

*I*n loving memory of my beloved daughter, Lisa Marie Rose, born on September 12, 1986, and taken from us just two weeks before her twentieth birthday. Her brief but impactful nineteen years with us left an indelible mark on our lives that we will forever cherish and hold close to our hearts.

CONTENTS

FOREWORD

*J*n the journey of faith, we often find ourselves navigating through the darkest valleys, grappling with the profound mysteries of suffering and loss. Yet it is in these moments of deepest anguish that the light of Christ shines most brightly, illuminating the path to healing and redemption.

In the pages of this extraordinary testament, you will encounter the courageous spirit of Cheryl, a beloved member of our parish family, whose journey through the depths of grief and heartache has been nothing short of miraculous.

The loss of a child to violence is a tragedy beyond comprehension—a wound that cuts to the very core of our being, leaving us reeling in pain and despair. Yet through the ministry of inner healing and deliverance, Cheryl discovered a reservoir of strength and grace that defied all earthly understanding.

As you read Cheryl's story, you will bear witness to the transformative power of forgiveness—a forgiveness born not of human strength, but of divine mercy. In the face of unspeakable evil, Cheryl chose to extend the same compassion and grace that she herself had received from her Savior, Christ Jesus. It is a testament to the radical love of God, which knows no bounds and offers healing to even the most shattered of hearts.

But Cheryl's journey is not merely a story of forgiveness; it is also a testament to the power of inner healing—a journey of reclaiming wholeness in the midst of brokenness. Through prayer, reflection, and the loving support of her faith community, Cheryl embarked on a path toward healing—a path illuminated by the gentle presence of the Holy Spirit and the promise of restoration found in Christ.

As you embark on this journey alongside Cheryl, may her story serve as a beacon of hope for all who find themselves walking through the valley of the shadow of death. May it remind us that, even in our darkest hour, we are never alone, for our Savior walks beside us, offering comfort, healing, and the promise of eternal life.

With prayerful anticipation,

Pastor Ulysis Velozo
Revelation Sphere Church

INTRODUCTION

*W*elcome to *Triumph over Tragedy: My Journey of Healing after My Daughter's Murder,* by Cheryl Ann Rottman. In this poignant true-life story, Cheryl shares her courageous and inspiring journey through the depths of grief, seeking healing and resilience after the devastating loss of her beloved daughter. Join her as she navigates the challenging path from despair to triumph, offering a testament to the human spirit's capacity for resilience and recovery in the face of unimaginable sorrow.

CHAPTER 1

ABOUT LISA

*A*s I reflect on the amazing day Lisa was born, I can't help but wonder why my husband and I waited five years to welcome her into our lives. She was a perfect baby, receiving a ten on her Apgar score. She weighed 6 pounds, 6.5 ounces and measured 19.5 inches long.

The first people at the hospital to welcome her into this world were her grandparents, Herbert and Marie Rose, along with her aunt and uncle, Jane and Richard Rose, and her Aunt Debbie. Lisa held a special place in the Rose family, as she was the first girl to be born in ten years. Her cousin, Amy, was the only girl among four boy cousins on the Rose family side; she was already ten years old at the time. On the Young side of the family, Lisa grew up surrounded by numerous cousins whom she loved dearly, too many to name individually.

I remember the drive home from the hospital like it was yesterday. Our eyes were fixed on this beautiful baby girl who had already captured our hearts.

I was overjoyed to hold her in my arms that day. I can still vividly recall the sensation of her soft, fragile form against my chest and the way my husband and I beamed with immense happiness, our cheeks aching from our endless smiles. We felt an unparalleled sense of contentment, knowing that this little bundle of joy was ours to cherish. Yet amid this profound joy, a knot of apprehension gnawed at my stomach as I contemplated how to navigate the unknown waters of motherhood.

As a new mother, I was stepping into an unfamiliar phase of my life, having missed the typical teenage experience of babysitting due to my upbringing in an orphanage in Austin, Texas, called the Junior Helping Hand Home for Children. During those early, uncertain days, our friends' and families' support and guidance were a lifeline.

One evening stands out in my memory, a night when Lisa's cries seemed relentless, having no discernible cause. We diligently checked to ensure she was well fed, clean, and comfortable. Yet her cries persisted, tugging at our hearts. Fear gripped me, as I was thinking about my own life—at the age of eighteen months, I had almost died from a ruptured appendix.

It was during this challenging moment that a dear friend, like a beacon of hope, shared a brilliant idea. She suggested placing a towel on our running dryer and gently laying Lisa on it. As I did, a remarkable transformation unfolded before my eyes!

The comforting hum and gentle vibrations from the dryer worked miraculously, gradually soothing my baby girl into a peaceful slumber. This ingenious solution quickly became a beloved routine that we relied on countless times.

My reminiscences here bring back pleasant memories.

As the seasons changed, so did our precious Lisa. She emerged from her fussy phase, gradually transforming before our eyes into the sweetest child. The memories of those early days—the sleepless nights and the constant care we provided for her—remain etched in my heart as a testament to the boundless love we held for our daughter.

Lisa was an extraordinary daughter, granddaughter, cousin, and friend, adored by all who knew her. She was witty, loving, kind, compassionate, and had an innate ability to connect with everyone she met. Her inner beauty matched her outer radiance.

Lisa's exuberant personality was reflected in her unwavering obsession with all things yellow. The mere glimpse of anything yellow would instantly illuminate her face with pure joy. Even a humble yellow pencil with smiley faces on it would make her beam from ear to ear. I can still hear her quirky and recognizable voice saying, "It's yellow," and then laughing.

Her grandparents held a special place in their hearts for her and affectionately called her "Lisa Pie." We spent almost every weekend at her grandparents' home so they could enjoy their granddaughter. Lisa's Aunt Kathy created a little yellow book in her honor, titled *A Girl Called Pie*, and presented it to us one Christmas after Lisa passed away. In this book, it describes how Lisa loved holidays, especially her favorite, Thanksgiving, at Aunt Kathy's house. It showed many photos of Lisa enjoying family events, church, school activities, and her dog, Petie.

Lisa's dad, Dusty, adored her and couldn't wait to hold and hug her every day after he got off work. He was a great dad, a reflection of his wonderful parents and upbringing. Family held immense significance for him, and as a result, we spent a lot of time cherishing community and family traditions.

I treasure all the photographs and videos of family gatherings, but there is one particular video that holds a special place in my heart. It was created by Lisa's uncle Richard Rose and captures her first two years of life. The two-hour video was presented to us as a heartfelt Christmas gift. Watching it now brings back cherished memories of family gatherings, joyous holidays, memorable birthdays, and the precious moments between cousins.

But things took a turn when Lisa was only eighteen months old. Her father was diagnosed with non-Hodgkin's lymphoma. He began an aggressive treatment of chemotherapy. Although he went into remission for almost two years, he later relapsed. He needed a bone marrow transplant, but no match was ever found. He tried experimental drugs, but the drugs just made him more ill. He was sick off and on for most of Lisa's young life. Her dad ended up in the hospital on her tenth birthday with fever and septicemia. I remember the doctor being very angry at me for not calling the paramedics sooner to get him to the hospital. I cried and felt horrible, hearing that he thought it was all my fault; but Dusty had not wanted to go to the hospital. He was there for about a week and then got to go home. A nurse came to the house every day for the next two weeks to give him antibiotic injections.

Unfortunately, just a couple of weeks later, he ended up in the hospital again with pancreatitis. Rod Young, Lisa's pastor at the time, came to visit him in the hospital and led him to the Lord before he passed away on October 18.

How does a ten-year-old grieve the loss of a parent? The day after her father's passing, Lisa went to school and shared about her loss as if it were show-and-tell.

It wasn't until much later that I discovered from several of her high school friends that she would drive to the graveyard where he was buried and talk to them about her dad. Everyone handles grief in their way. I was fortunate to have the support of a loving family and a caring community of Christians from my church, who were there for me whenever I needed someone to lean on.

Lisa had a multitude of friends, all of whom she cherished equally. However, there was one friend in particular whom she held closest to her heart, as they had been inseparable since their kindergarten days all the way through high school. This cherished friend was none other than Katie Morris Alvarez, affectionately known as "Katie Mo" by Lisa. It was Lisa who bestowed this nickname upon Katie, and in return, Katie lovingly dubbed Lisa "Lisa Mo." Their bond grew stronger with each passing year, and they shared countless memories—from sleepovers to birthday parties to school dances. Eventually they proudly walked the stage together at the Richard King High School graduation. The friendship between Lisa and Katie was truly a gift they both cherished.

Lisa was the kind of person who could brighten up a room just by walking in. She had a natural gift for making everyone feel welcome, whether they were new students in school or new faces at church. Her sincere aversion to seeing anyone unhappy led her to do silly things to bring laughter, like her favorite "ET" walk or her repertoire of funny faces.

From a young age, she excelled at swimming, beginning at the age of three. She started piano lessons at five and continued until she graduated from high school. She also played the violin and sang at church. Although she loved sports, her true passion lay in being with her friends and cheering them on. Yes, my Lisa was a special and unique individual.

Lisa went on mission trips to Mexico and New York with Pastor Miguel Santoyo, his family, and their youth group. She would tell me about her adventures, especially her trips to the slums and the orphanage. Lisa's extroverted nature set her apart, revealing a unique personality trait.

Her genuine concern for others was evident in her strong desire to care for all the young children she encountered. Rather than attending youth services, she often chose to dedicate her time to helping in the church nursery. She would eagerly bring the children home with her if she could, showcasing her unwavering love for them.

She had lofty aspirations and dreams, including completing her college education to become a preschool teacher with a dual major in American Sign Language. She firmly believed in marrying one day and having a family of four children, even choosing names for the two boys and two girls she intended to have. Tragically, Lisa's life was cut short, and none of these dreams were realized. Despite her short time on earth—only nineteen years—I am truly blessed to have had her in my life. The numerous photographs and videos of her are now cherished memories that I hold dear.

Lisa didn't always make the right choices when it came to relationships. She had a nurturing spirit, always trying to bring people to church and help them find their way. Yet she knew that it was only God who could truly reach the lost and hurting. Her favorite thing to say, which she learned at church, was "Believe the best in everyone."

Though fleeting, Lisa's life is a profound testament to the enduring forces of love, compassion, and faith. Her memory serves as a wellspring of inspiration for all who had the privilege of knowing her, and her impact on the world stands as an enduring legacy that will be cherished eternally.

Life goes on…

I was a widow for three years and then met Douglas Rottman. As of the writing of this book in 2024, we are about to celebrate twenty-five years of marriage. Doug has three children, but only one the same age as Lisa. His name is Christopher, and he and Lisa had a very close bond. From the time they were thirteen, they spent every other weekend together at our home. Lisa was so excited to have a brother. They would swim in the pool, go to movies, go to the mall, or hang out together for hours and talk about everything.

Doug and Lisa bonded nicely too. I remember when Doug and I would sit down to watch TV together, Lisa had to be sitting right in the middle of us. She longed to have a father-daughter relationship once again. Although they didn't always see eye to eye on many things, there was special love between them.

The last time Lisa attended church was a couple of months before she passed away. I remember that day as if it were yesterday. It was Mother's Day, and she brought her boyfriend with her.

His inner turmoil manifested in a storm of profanity during the church service, and Lisa's valiant attempts to silence him proved futile. I keenly sensed a spiritual conflict brewing, and though I couldn't decipher the words that passed between them, Lisa later recounted the turbulent exchange to me. It was no surprise, for it was evident that a profound battle raged for his soul. Regrettably, this marked a turning point in Lisa's life, leading to darker days that the forthcoming chapters will reveal. I often find myself contemplating what more Lisa might have done for her boyfriend and others, but in times like these, we're reminded of the ways in which God works and the choices people make in their lives.

CHAPTER 2

THE KNOCK AT THE DOOR

*I*t was a quiet morning on Wednesday, August 30, 2006, the clock striking precisely 8:30 a.m. The serenity of my existence was shattered by a sudden, booming knock at the front door. I cautiously approached the door, peeking out the side window to identify the unexpected visitor. To my astonishment, a solemn figure stood on my doorstep clad in a police officer's uniform.

Initially I entertained the idea that this was a case of mistaken identity, a mix-up that had led him to my doorstep. However, as he introduced himself, his name and appearance faded into the background, drowned by the emotions that were about to engulf me.

The officer's inquiry about a yellow Dodge Neon, a vehicle registered in my name but belonging to my daughter, Lisa, sent a shiver down my spine.

The weight of his words became evident as he disclosed that she had been involved in a shooting at Janet's Cakery, the bakery where she worked. My heart raced as he inquired about the potential driver of the car, and with fear, I mentioned her boyfriend, Chris Quartaro, as a possible suspect.

The police officer revealed that a high-speed chase involving the vehicle was already underway. Calmly he advised my husband and I to make our way to the bakery, allowing us to set our own pace.

While Doug and I prepared to leave the house that day, there was a nervous apprehension that took over me. With a sense of determination still mingled with apprehension, we hastily prepared ourselves before embarking on the fifteen-minute drive to the bakery, bracing ourselves for the unknown that lay ahead.

The police officer had only given us sketchy details about the shooting. As we reached our destination, the bakery was cordoned off with yellow caution tape, and the atmosphere was thick with tears. I couldn't fathom why everyone around me was weeping. Approaching one of Lisa's friends, I anxiously inquired about her whereabouts, only to be met with disbelief in her response: "You mean you don't know?"

Confused and anxious, I implored her to explain. With a heavy heart, she disclosed that Lisa had been shot by Chris and had been rushed to the trauma center at Spohn Memorial Hospital in an ambulance.

I was in total disbelief and shock. My world was immediately shattered. "Lisa…shot," I mumbled as her friend said it was so. Tears streamed down her face. *No, this had to be a dream, a bad dream!* I thought as all the noise around me immediately fell silent.

My baby girl can't be gone so soon, I thought, more frantic than ever. Just the night before, she had come over to use my computer and register for her third semester at college. Thoughts raced through my mind, desperately hoping that this couldn't be true.

The police officer who had visited our home had only mentioned a shooting, omitting the fact that Lisa had been shot and the severity of her injury.

In that critical moment, time seemed to slow to a crawl, and a profound numbness washed over me, leaving me in a state of shock. My heart raced, and my thoughts grew hazy. How could this unimaginable tragedy have unfolded? The person I held most dear, my daughter, had been shot by her boyfriend. It was at that moment that a flood of thoughts and regrets inundated my mind: if only I had known; if only I could have seen it coming. Countless "what-ifs" raced through my consciousness.

CHAPTER 3

AT THE HOSPITAL

*A*s my husband drove us to the hospital, which was a good thirty minutes away, I began making phone calls to inform friends, family, and our pastor of the dire situation. Thankfully many of them rushed to the hospital to offer their support.

However, despite our eagerness, we were not allowed to see her in the emergency room, which left me pacing the floor anxiously. The reason behind the delay remains a mystery to me.

Eventually we were granted permission to enter the emergency room, and as I approached Lisa, I was taken aback by her unrecognizable appearance. Her face was severely swollen. A white turban had been placed on her head to control the bleeding, but blood continued to trickle from her nose and mouth. I felt a profound sense of disbelief and helplessness, as if I were looking at someone else's child instead of my own.

I held Lisa's hand tightly as I trembled, and tears streamed down my face. I desperately prayed. My sister-in-law, Debbie, urged me to speak louder, to let her hear me. Despite the pain in my heart of seeing my Lisa this way, I lifted my voice and continued to pray. Then our pastor joined in, his prayers filled with enthusiasm, hoping for a speedy recovery and a miraculous turnaround. I can vividly recall the pastor's words, "Where there is breath, there is life," as he pressed on with his prayers.

Suddenly, the medical staff abruptly instructed us to leave the emergency room as paramedics rushed in with another patient who had suffered a gunshot wound. To our utter shock, it was Chris. Confusion engulfed me as I wondered why they were bringing him here.

We had learned he had led the police on a dangerous high-speed chase spanning three counties using Lisa's car. In the end, the sheriff successfully turned off the vehicle by shooting out its tires, forcing it to come to a halt on a bridge very close to an elementary school. It was at this harrowing juncture that, in an act of desperation, Chris turned the gun on himself. The bullet entered through his mouth and exited through his forehead. Years later I heard another story saying that the gun went off accidentally, but I don't really believe that. You see, Chris was supposed to be in court the following Monday for an assault charge against his mother. More details are in the subsequent chapters.

As plans were in motion to relocate Lisa to the ICU on another floor, once again we found ourselves caught in the waiting game for several hours. The arrival of more friends, family members, and another pastor friend consoled us, and they asked if there was anything they could do. All I could think of saying was to please pray for a miracle.

Urgent surgery was immediately performed to save Chris's life while my daughter's life teetered on the precipice. My daughter was the victim of this tragic ordeal and in desperate need of immediate attention. However, the gravity of her condition didn't truly hit me until a second doctor emerged and conveyed that there were no further options for her—the bullet had gone in near her temple, and there was no brain activity.

"I'm sorry." The doctor's voice trembled as she uttered those words before quietly retreating down the corridor.

I felt my heart shatter into countless pieces, and I was overwhelmed by shock. How could I possibly continue living with such a devastating loss?

My close friend, who was by my side, shared in my grief and confided in me that she, too, was at a loss for words and actions in the face of such profound sorrow. "You're a strong woman," my friend kept reassuring me. She said that I would be fine because I was a woman of great faith. I certainly didn't feel like a strong woman, but instead felt my heart was broken into pieces. I thought about what some Christians say and still use to this day: "God won't give us more than you can handle." But that is untrue, unhelpful, and certainly not biblical. That statement is man-centered and not God-centered. In times like these, we must learn to lean on the Lord for strength; I was holding on by a thread.

At that moment, I made the heart-wrenching decision to visit Lisa alone one last time. It was already three o'clock in the afternoon when I entered the ICU room, where a nurse was attending to her.

Overwhelmed with helplessness and numbness, I mustered the courage to express my confusion to the nurse. She reassured me that Lisa was not experiencing any pain and that it was OK to let her go. How could I possibly bring myself to do that? A part of me resisted, but I knew I had to bid her farewell. Lisa passed away a few minutes after I left the room.

It was undoubtedly the most agonizing day of my life. Even though I'd endured numerous hardships in my life, this was by far the most devastating. Never could I have imagined that my only child would be taken from me in such a tragic, heartbreaking manner. Parents should outlive their children, not the other way around. It should never be this way.

As Doug and I left the hospital, we were faced with the painful task of informing our family and friends about Lisa's death. The thought weighed heavily on my heart. How could I possibly find the strength to tell all those who loved her of this devastating news? It felt like an impossible task, but I knew I had to summon every ounce of courage within me to face this excruciating duty. Lisa's memory deserved to be honored, and those who cared for her deserved to know of her passing.

The weight of that news was a crushing burden, a stark reminder of just how fragile life truly is. It forced me to confront the fact that every day is a precious gift from God, and we must never take our loved ones for granted. The importance of expressing our love and appreciation to them every single day became painfully clear.

As the sun rose on the second day following Lisa's tragic passing, the world around me appeared as a hazy blur. The profound shock of losing her had exacted an immense toll on my body, leaving me unable to stomach even a morsel of food. All I longed for was the presence of my dear Lisa, and during those moments, I would have given anything to have her back by my side.

Each day felt like an impossible struggle as I grappled with the overwhelming pain that seemed to have settled deep within me. In the middle of this all-encompassing sorrow, there was one task I couldn't avoid and still hadn't done—the agonizing duty of reaching out to friends and family to convey the heart-wrenching news of Lisa's untimely departure.

But there was no escaping it; I had to do it.

With a trembling heart, I called family, friends, and coworkers, one after another, and as soon as they picked up, I heard them utter the simple word "Hello?" My voice quavered as I recounted the tragic events, and with each word, a wellspring of empathy poured forth from the other end of the line. All of them were in complete disbelief and utter shock.

Every phone call served as a poignant reminder of the immense void that Lisa's absence had carved into our lives.

A dear friend who had known Lisa since childhood offered her condolences, saying, "I can't believe she's gone. She was such a bright light in this world."

Another friend, choking back tears, said, "I'll always remember her laughter and the way she could make anyone smile, even on the darkest days."

Through the cloud of loss and despair, it was evident that life as I knew it had altered irreversibly. The grief of losing my beautiful daughter was unlike any other. It was echoed by the quiet moments of our house, which was now filled with memories and a terrible emptiness.

Amid this heart-wrenching ordeal, Chris emerged from surgery. He remained in the hospital for a week under constant police supervision. Eventually he was transferred to jail, where he would await his sentencing and trial.

I felt a sense of relief when Chris was finally incarcerated. As the shock and grief enveloped me, I couldn't help but wonder if I would ever find it within myself to forgive him for what he had done to my only child. The conflicting emotions of anger, pain, and a desire for justice swirled within me, making forgiveness seem like an impossible mountain to climb.

CHAPTER 4

THE FUNERAL

The process of preparing a funeral for my only child was daunting. I was completely lost in the world of arranging funeral preparations. Thankfully my two sisters-in-law, Kathy and Debbie, came to my aid, providing support and advice.

As we sat down to examine the specifics, an overpowering sensation of sadness and emptiness dominated the room. The questions I never imagined I'd have to answer loomed before me: Who will officiate the service? Who would be the pallbearers for Lisa's casket? Where were we going to bury her? The weight of these decisions weighed heavily on me, and my mind fought to grasp the enormity of it all.

Honestly, there's no deeper pain than laying your child to rest.

The process of selecting a coffin proved to be excruciating. Stepping into the room filled with an array of beautiful caskets felt strangely unsettling. The atmosphere was cold and sterile, a stark contrast to the warmth and joy my daughter had once brought into our lives and the lives of everyone she met.

Tears streamed down my cheeks as I roamed, inspecting each casket, searching for one that felt less cold and more inviting. Most were stainless steel, but one stood out in the midst of metal—a beautiful, warm, stained-wood coffin. Spending thousands on something so exquisite only to lay it six feet under felt like a terrible waste.

With that matter resolved, we turned our attention to other issues. Doug knew the florist at the funeral, and we met with her to choose everything in yellow, to reflect her joyous attitude and personality.

Now it was time to choose an outfit for Lisa to wear at her funeral. The perfect ensemble came to mind—a yellow top, a long black skirt, and tennis shoes, her favorite church attire. However, when I brought her clothes to the mortician, she gently explained that it wouldn't be suitable. I didn't quite understand why.

She explained that Lisa had bruises all over her body, and if we wanted an open-casket funeral, we needed to dress her in garments that covered her arms and neck. Devastated, I dashed to the nearest department store, tears flowing down my cheeks, feverishly looking for acceptable apparel. I know I looked strange that day because everybody around me kept glancing at me with immense pity.

Eventually I found a long-sleeved white shirt and a yellow bandanna to cover her neck. The mortician dressed Lisa in these clothes, but we still felt dissatisfied with her appearance. In a final attempt to honor her beauty, the mortician suggested draping a beautiful white-lace veil over the opening of the casket. Once she placed the white-lace veil over the opening, we were satisfied.

Friends and family gathered for the viewing to remember Lisa and share stories of her short life. The shock of her passing still lingered heavily, and I found myself simply going through the motions, unable to process the reality of it all fully.

The funeral was held on Labor Day in 2006, a day filled with a mixture of sorrow and holiday festivities. The parlor was filled with an array of gorgeous flower arrangements. One caught my eye—it was made up of over fifty lovely yellow roses and sent by Dusty's best friend, Danny Sanchez.

Our pastor, Miguel Santoyo, a guiding light in Lisa's life, led the heartfelt service. Mickey, his son, and the worship team played songs that had held a special place in Lisa's heart, filling the room with nostalgia and sorrow.

Still in shock, I cried silently. Beside me, Doug fought to hold back his emotions, but I knew deep down that we were both drowning in sadness and despair. Our vibrant Lisa, the essence of our lives, was gone forever.

The funeral was packed, with standing room only. Many guests in the rear stood for more than two hours to pay their respects to Lisa and to support our bereaved family. It was proof of her significant influence on the lives of people around her.

During the service, many of Lisa's closest friends took the opportunity to share their memories and express how she had touched their lives. One friend in particular spoke about how Lisa fearlessly shared her faith in Jesus, never hesitating to proclaim the message of salvation boldly. It was this friend who once received Lisa's invitation to know Jesus, and who now serves the Lord alongside her husband. It was a powerful reminder of Lisa's lasting impact on those she encountered.

As the service ended, a bittersweet atmosphere permeated the air. Although we were grateful for the chance to commemorate Lisa's life and her lasting impact, the stark reality of her absence was still a jolting shock that we were all grappling to accept. Our hearts heavy and our emotions swirling, we couldn't escape the intense yearning for Lisa's comforting presence.

Tears flowed from every eye as the funeral director closed the casket. The pallbearers solemnly carried Lisa's lifeless body to her final resting place, right beside her dad's grave. The pain felt by everyone present was almost too much to bear.

At the grave site, Pastor Miguel closed with a prayer. In a heartfelt moment, one of Lisa's high school friends, who had been in orchestra class with her, shared a song on his violin. It wasn't the most polished performance, but it was the sentiment behind it that truly mattered. He recalled how Lisa often told him that he needed to practice more, even though she didn't mean it unkindly. We all shared a lighthearted laugh, as that was just Lisa—someone who spoke her mind without filter. It was a special memory I'll hold dear to my heart.

As Lisa was laid to rest, soil covering her, a sharp pang hit my chest, and I cried out, realizing it wasn't a dream, hurting even more.

We returned to the graveyard many times over the next few years, but a tremendous sense of emptiness remained. Gradually I found myself only attending on special occasions, such as her birthday or on holidays.

Since our move to Florida, I have been unable to visit the graveyard physically, but happily, I have friends who graciously take flowers there on our behalf.

To remember the value of life, I now buy flowers for my home to remind myself that they are intended for the living rather than the departed. Also, Doug planted a special plumeria in our backyard called the "Lisa Marie." It's one of a kind just like our Lisa!

CHAPTER 5

THE TRIAL

Chris was incarcerated in Nueces County, where we resided, and the thought of spending the holidays with him nearby was unbearable. Determined to seek solace, I picked up the phone and reached out to others, asking for their prayers for a swift and speedy trial. Miraculously our prayers were answered, and within two months, the trial was set and ready to go.

Murder trials are notoriously lengthy proceedings, but in this case, it was concluded in just two days, resulting in Chris being convicted and handed a life sentence. He was subsequently transferred to a prison far from our vicinity. Naively, I believed that his relocation would bring me peace, but the next chapter of my life would prove otherwise. In the following chapter, I will share the details of that tumultuous journey.

Throughout the two-day trial, we listened to the testimonies of witnesses from the bakery. We were informed about the recent purchase of a gun by Chris right before Lisa was tragically shot. We heard the testimony from the security guard, who was not actually on duty that day. He and Lisa had talked many times. She had told him of the abuse she had experienced and showed him the many bruises on her body.

Additionally, we were informed about the distressing accounts of physical abuse that Lisa had endured. More details of this abuse will follow in another chapter.

In another testimony we heard about Chris's mistreatment of Lisa's innocent new puppy, Deuce. As I sat there absorbing all this distressing information, I felt as though I were an outsider, observing someone else's trial. The experience was akin to being lost in a hazy fog or a dream.

At the conclusion of the trial, just moments before the jury delivered their verdict, I was given the opportunity to address Chris during the victim impact panel. Instead of expressing my true feelings, which were anger and contempt toward him, I chose to announce my decision to forgive him. This choice was deeply rooted in my faith as a believer in Jesus rather than being influenced by my emotions.

"Chris, I chose to forgive you for what you did; I know Lisa would have done the same."

He remained silent and unresponsive. Later I discovered that his mouth had been wired shut due to the gunshot wound and the subsequent surgery he had undergone.

As I made my way back to my seat, I could feel my emotions rise once more. I began shaking, but I needed to remain calm and strong. The verdict came after a very brief recess, and he was sentenced for first degree murder, with life in prison plus two years for evading arrest using a vehicle.

But the question now was, did I really forgive Chris?

CHAPTER 6

THE LONG JOURNEY

*O*ver time, the traumatic event inflicted immense suffering upon me, manifesting as haunting nightmares, lapses in memory, debilitating panic attacks, and an overwhelming sense of fear. For nearly three years, I couldn't even drive along the street where the bakery was located without feeling overwhelmed with rage, despair, and other powerful emotions. The ache returned, impacting every fiber of my existence.

Some may claim that this is a natural part of the mourning process, and to some extent, it is. However, when we choose not to forgive or allow bitterness to take root fully, problems begin to surface.

Watching television shows, the news, or movies with violence or guns became difficult for me. I went out of my way to avoid running into people I knew at the grocery store, opting to take a different route if I spotted them.

Attending church and teaching children's ministry became things of the past. Instead, I started working excessively, putting in fifty hours a week, solely to keep myself occupied and distract myself from the emotional distress I was experiencing. I knew I was quickly becoming a social outcast.

The torment grew even more intense when I discovered that Chris had no memory of the horrifying events that had occurred that day. The burden of holding onto unforgiveness, bitterness, anger, resentment, hatred, hurt, and pain started to overwhelm and consume me, wreaking havoc on my life. The intense weight of these emotions became so unbearable that I even contemplated ending my own life.

This marked the beginning of a significant setback in my spiritual and life journey. I started experiencing excruciating pain throughout my body, from the top of my head to the soles of my feet. I attributed it to the long work hours I spent walking and standing on my feet each day, but I soon realized it was much deeper than physical pain. The choice to withhold forgiveness brings torment upon us, as told in the Bible. Who are these tormentors? They are the demons that hold us captive in the prison of our souls.

But how does one forgive someone who doesn't recall their actions? Forgiveness is a personal journey that doesn't depend on the other person's memory. However, I couldn't help but wonder why he didn't remember. As mentioned before, he had attempted suicide (so I thought) by turning the gun on himself. The bullet had passed through his mouth and exited through the top of his forehead, resulting in partial memory loss.

When I confronted him during the trial, it felt like I had forgiven him. It was a deliberate choice—I knew it was the right path. But in hindsight, I see I was in shock, merely following the motions.

After the trial, I discovered more shocking details about the extent of Lisa's physical and emotional abuse, and it reignited my anger toward Chris and others. It felt like a never-ending cycle of torment. One day, while Lisa's friends were gathered at my house, they began discussing the physical and emotional abuse she had endured. They had urged her to leave Chris, but she believed she could somehow fix his problems. I remembered Lisa mentioning that she thought having Chris write in a journal might be therapeutic for him, just as it had helped her in the past. Little did she know that this would only worsen the situation.

I learned about some of the physical abuse during the trial, but later I discovered the extent of what she had endured. Surprisingly enough, as I've heard, Lisa had asked everyone to keep it a secret from me and my husband. Lisa and I had always shared a close bond and spoke regularly, so I couldn't comprehend why she didn't want me to know. When I saw Lisa the night before the shooting, she had said nothing. It was a very short visit, as Chris was with her, pacing the floor and going in and out of the house. I had asked him if he wanted a chair to sit next to her, and he said no. I thought it was odd that he kept going in and out of the house. Did he have the gun in the car at that time? This was the last time I got to hug my daughter and tell her I loved her.

More recently I learned about the ongoing physical abuse from one of Lisa's friends, who was the ex-girlfriend of Chris. She had warned Lisa that he would be fine for a while but then would fly off the handle and abuse her and disappear for days, only to go back later and apologize and try to mend the relationship. Things were very good for a couple of months with Chris and Lisa, but then Chris began having violent outbursts—hitting her, damaging her car, and leaving for days. Many times, Lisa would have to walk to work or try to get a ride. I was told that employees at her job saw the many large bruises on her legs and arms, and they questioned her, but she would not admit it was Chris. But they all knew.

Her friend had told her enough was enough, and that they should go to her parents now. Lisa had said she absolutely did not want her parents to know anything at all because we would not listen, and she could not go home. But that was an absolute lie! She was always welcome at the house. We did tell her one time that Chris was not welcome because he disrespected Doug, but we would have never told her she couldn't come back home.

It was baffling to me why she would protect a man who was inflicting harm upon her. Why would she tolerate such despicable, unpredictable, and destructive behavior? I found it incredibly challenging to grasp the reasons behind her actions. One evening while my husband and I had been out for dinner, Lisa had called, crying, to say that Chris had spit on her. I told her that she didn't need to put up with that abuse. She said later that he'd apologized to her.

On another occasion she came to visit me at my job wearing a turtleneck sweater in the middle of summer. I learned later that she was wearing the sweater to cover her neck because Chris had tried to strangle her and left marks. Then I began beating myself up for not recognizing the signs of abuse.

Lisa had fallen into the role of a victim, trapped in a mentality that perpetuated her suffering. Despite her unrelenting efforts to improve her situation, Chris relentlessly tore her down through verbal, emotional, and even physical abuse. And my poor Lisa tolerated it all.

One of Lisa's friends gave this advice: "If I were helping someone today, I would advise them to reach out to the family or close relatives of their friend, coworker, neighbor, etcetera if I noticed them going through something like this. It's important to try to get help as soon as possible. I know it's hard to see past the trauma bond. I also know now that any mother, relative, or friend would cherish the chance to assist their child or someone's child in escaping a challenging circumstance, rather than having to bury them and mourn the loss. I regret not taking different actions back then, and it took me a considerable amount of time to even forgive myself."

In writing this book, my sincere hope and prayer is for women trapped in abusive relationships to discover the divine strength within themselves, empowering them to seek assistance and liberate themselves from the grip of their abusers. It is of utmost importance to grasp that permitting another person to shatter your spirit and overall well-being is never acceptable.

CHAPTER 7

QUEST FOR HEALING

$\mathcal{F}$ive long years had passed since the heart-wrenching loss of my beloved daughter, Lisa. On an ordinary day while unloading groceries outside my home, my neighbor from down the street, Dee deShetler, couldn't help but notice the bright-yellow ribbon carefully tied in a bow around a branch of our Chinese tallow tree. Her curiosity got the best of her, and she inquired about its significance.

With a sad heart, I told the heartbreaking story behind the yellow ribbon, describing how it represented the awful tragedy at Janet's that had taken my daughter's life. Every year I would ornament the tree with a new ribbon to symbolize my unending love and devotion for Lisa.

"That's heartbreaking. Lisa was an absolute gem."

"Thank you, Dee." My eyes were filled with tears by then. And all Dee could do was look at me compassionately. She couldn't possibly pacify me by this time, but I believed she wondered how she could. Dee had known Lisa from the bakery; Lisa had worked there briefly and had a deep connection with the customers.

That day Dee extended an invitation for me to join her Bible study group down at the library on Fridays. I needed some time to think about the idea. After about a year, I finally made up my mind to attend. In the beginning I sat there silently, tears flowing as I grappled with my brokenness, grief, and pain. Over time I began to meet with Dee privately for ministry sessions, engaging in lengthy conversations over lunch.

In 2011 Dee commenced an eight-week course called "There Is Healing in Deliverance," tailored for individuals seeking relief from emotional and physical pain. At that point I was in profound torment, and this teaching seemed like the perfect fit, even though I hadn't fully grasped the term "deliverance" just yet. I'll delve into its meaning in more detail shortly.

I've mentioned the yellow ribbon on the tree branch in my front yard. Let me paint a clearer picture of what was happening to that branch. It was slowly shedding its bark, one layer at a time, a process that would eventually consume the branch entirely.

I finally removed the ribbon from the branch, allowing it to thrive again. This branch reflected my inner self withering away, affecting me physically, emotionally, and spiritually.

I endured excruciating pain from my back down to my feet, all stemming from a toxic blend of unforgiveness, resentment, bitterness, anger, guilt, complicated grief, hurt, and pain. Desperate for relief, I sought solace in natural remedies like chiropractic care, massages, and exercise, but these were only fleeting fixes. I was trapped in my self-made prison.

When trapped in a self-made prison, it's strange how a part of you can almost relish the captivity. That's what was happening to me, and I was aware it was all wrong, but it felt like I had no way out.

Lisa and I had shared a close-knit, beautiful relationship full of dreams and love. When I lost her, my world came crashing down. Not only were my hopes and dreams shattered, but so were Lisa's. She'd been a student at Del Mar College, studying to become a teacher. She had dreamed of marriage and a family, but that dream was cut short.

Her life was tragically taken by a man she believed she could help. Despite her friends' warnings to get away from him because he posed a lethal threat, I don't believe she could have fathomed the horror that lay ahead.

The primary aspect of inner healing is healing the dissociated or fragmented parts of the soul, which consist of your mind, will, and emotions. This profound life journey of soul restoration and transformation is only possible through the leading of the Holy Spirit and brought to Jesus for healing, as our great physician, healer, and deliverer. It's a true miracle, not easily understood until one personally experiences the supernatural healing power of Jesus.

On the other hand, deliverance involves the expulsion of spiritual darkness and oppression from our lives. The ministry of deliverance is supernatural. Jesus came to set us free from evil spirits, torment, pain, sin, sickness, etcetera, and He has given us the authority as believers to do the same. The Bible declares this in Luke 4:18 (NKJV): "The Spirit of the Lord is upon me, because he has anointed me to preach the gospel to the poor; he has sent me to heal the brokenhearted, to preach deliverance to the captives, and recovering of sight to the blind, to set at liberty them that are bruised."

These intertwined processes are essential for our overall well-being and spiritual growth. My voyage toward inner healing has been an enduring and often challenging path spanning numerous years.

In my quest for inner healing and deliverance, I realized the need to break the self-inflicted curses born from my own words. There was a time when my expressions painted a bleak picture of my heart, one marked by nineteen figurative stab wounds. I even went so far as to regret the birth of my child, since I now knew she would live only until the age of nineteen. I eventually recognized that such negative thoughts and declarations were a contradiction to the divine gift of life bestowed by God Himself.

As life carried me forward, I encountered new layers of inner turmoil, despair, and heartbreak. I believed that relocating to Florida, far from the place where my beloved Lisa had grown up, would be a fresh start—running away from my own shadow, as some would put it. There is such a thing as a location-change mentality—it is an attempt to overcome issues by physically moving to a new location. The problem was I was using carnal means to crush the demonic, and it didn't work. One day I went to the courthouse shortly after we moved to Florida, and I had a major anxiety attack. I'm not saying that it's never a good idea to transfer to a new geographic place, however. Sometimes, moving is a good step in beginning a new season in your life. You must remember that shifting to a new location doesn't heal the heart or expel demons.

I fervently sought guidance from the Lord through prayer, hoping to find someone who could assist me in my quest for further healing of my tormented soul. During this time, the divine hand of the Lord led me to Invicta Ministries, a ministry of healing and deliverance under the compassionate leadership of Pastor Mark and Jana Chase in Fort Lauderdale. Through a series of sessions with Pastor Mark, my journey of healing and restoration continued.

Often the traumas we experience in life inadvertently unlock doors that house unresolved issues from our past, usually stemming from childhood. I had once naively believed that accepting Christ into my life would magically resolve all these deeply rooted problems and free me from the inner demons I harbored. However, my understanding evolved as I realized that the Bible teaches a more complex process of healing and deliverance, one that needs faith in all its spheres.

At the culmination of my journey, I received a divine message that resonated within my soul.

The voice of the Lord posed a pivotal question: "Are you ready to embrace forgiveness?" He gently reminded me that I didn't have to bear the weight of my struggles alone and that I had suffered long enough. It was time to surrender everything to Him and complete my journey toward healing.

I responded to His call, saying, "I am ready, Lord." I share this prayer today with the hope that it may offer solace and guidance to others:

Heavenly Father, in the name of Jesus and with the guidance of the Holy Spirit, I humbly repent and seek forgiveness. I choose to forgive those who have caused pain, including Chris, Lisa's friends, and those who knew of the abuse. I also choose to forgive myself. I lay my heartache, hurt, pain, and grief at the feet of the cross of Jesus. I ask for Your blessings upon these individuals, releasing them to You. In Jesus's name, I pray, amen.

This forgiveness was a conscious decision of my will, guided by the Holy Spirit, not contingent on fleeting emotions. As I sealed this prayer, I also remembered the wisdom in Matthew 6:14–15 (NKJV): "For if you forgive others their trespasses, your Heavenly Father will also forgive you; but if you do not forgive others their trespasses, neither will your Father forgive your trespasses." Unforgiveness is a spiritual stumbling block that can significantly hinder our connection with God.

May this shared journey of healing and forgiveness touch the hearts of those who read it, offering hope and guidance in their path to inner healing, restoration, and deliverance.

CONCLUSION

Triumph over Tragedy is a deeply inspiring book that reaches out to the hearts of those who have suffered the profound loss of a loved one, offering a ray of hope and the promise of healing. It is a beacon for those who have endured the anguish of trauma and abuse, a guiding light for anyone who feels imprisoned by their past. While I respect the value of secular counseling, I wholeheartedly believe that true healing comes only through biblical counseling, inner healing, and deliverance through Jesus alone.

In my journey I've been blessed by the unwavering support of countless individuals who have walked alongside me during my healing process. With God's loving assistance, anyone can embark on their unique journey toward inner healing, mending the shattered pieces of the heart left fragmented by trauma, pain, hurt, or grief.

This book is a testament to the resilience of the human spirit and the transformative power of faith.

It is a reminder that no matter how dark our past may be, there is always a path to healing, and that path is illuminated by the love and grace of our Savior, Jesus Christ. Together, we can move from tragedy to victory, emerging stronger and more whole than we ever thought possible.

ACKNOWLEDGMENTS

I give all glory and honor to God for allowing me to share my journey with the world. But I also want to express my deepest gratitude to a few extraordinary individuals. Each of them has played an indispensable role in my life's journey, and I feel compelled to share their impact with you.

To start with…

I want to express my heartfelt gratitude to my husband, Douglas, for his constant support and encouragement throughout our twenty-four years of marriage. He has consistently been my rock, providing a listening ear and acting as a sounding board. His unwavering strength and, most importantly, his presence during challenging times offered invaluable support, particularly in the face of the profound loss of Lisa. For at least three years, I found myself crying quite frequently and at a loss for hope, and he demonstrated remarkable patience and love as he held me and reassured me that we would overcome this together.

Prophet Ken Jackson, founder of Maintain Anointing Deliverance Ministries, crossed my path during an event in West Palm Beach, Florida back in 2018. His prophecy that "you shall write your book" proved to be a pivotal catalyst, propelling me to share my story with the world. I'm truly humbled and thankful for the Lord's confirmation and guidance through Prophet Ken's prophetic message.

Apostle Ulysis Velozo, affectionately known as Pastor U, has been a constant presence in my life, serving as my pastor, teacher, and counselor for many years. My journey with him included being a student in his on-line school, the Proton Believers Ministry Training School. During our time together, he generously imparted wisdom from the Bible, prayed fervently for me, prophesied over my life, and spoke to my circumstances. Today I feel incredibly blessed to be part of his church, Revelation Sphere Ministries, and an online chat called Divine Intervention.

I was deeply moved at a certain time when Pastor Ulysis placed the tallit (prayer shawl) over me and spoke the Father's blessing during a church ceremony. It felt like a divine embrace, deeply assuring me of God's pleasure and love as His cherished daughter.

Dee deShetler, an exceptional individual from Remnant Hope Center, entered my life when hope appeared to be in short supply. She became my Bible teacher, mentor, and deliverance minister—a role of profound significance. Our bond has grown over the years, and I now proudly call her a dear friend. During my darkest moments, especially after the tragic loss of my daughter, Dee dedicated countless hours to ministering to me. Finding a friend who consistently listens, offers support, and never once dismisses my needs due to a lack of time is rare. The gratitude I feel toward her is boundless, a reflection of her unwavering and unconditional love. She is a true woman of God, willing to sacrifice for others.

Pastor Mark Chase, the founder of Invicta Ministries of Inner Healing and Deliverance, entered my life when I moved to Florida in 2013. Recognizing the need for further healing and deliverance, I sought Pastor Mark's guidance. Through a series of life-changing counseling and inner healing sessions with him, I embarked on a transformative journey. Inspired by his teachings and mentorship, I am now enrolled in Invicta

University, pursuing my calling to help other women in addressing their issues of hurt, pain, trauma, and grief. Pastor Mark's evident influence on my life has been immeasurable, and I am eternally grateful for his guidance and support.

I share these acknowledgments with you, dear reader, to highlight the profound impact these remarkable individuals have had on my life's journey. Their support, wisdom, and love have shaped my path and made me who I am today.

ABOUT THE AUTHOR

*C*heryl Ann Rottman, the author of this book, is currently pursuing her education at Invicta University of Inner Healing and Deliverance, a respected ministry led by Pastors Mark and Jana Chase. Here, Cheryl is actively expanding her knowledge and honing her inner healing and deliverance skills under the guidance and tutelage of seasoned mentors.

Moreover, Cheryl has earned certification from Proton Believers Ministry Training School under the esteemed leadership of Pastor Ulysis Velozo. Her commitment to continuous learning and professional development is a testament to her dedication to the practice of inner healing and deliverance.

Cheryl's expertise in this field is not just theoretical but deeply rooted in her journey, one marked by the profound loss of her beloved daughter, Lisa Rose. Over the years, she has actively engaged in her healing process, seeking counseling, inner healing, and divine deliverance. This firsthand experience has ignited her passion to reach out to women who have faced the heart-wrenching loss of a child or have grappled with various forms of grief, pain, hurt, trauma, or abuse.

Cheryl's mission is to offer unwavering support and compassionate guidance to those who are in need, ultimately empowering them to embark on their journey of healing and restoration. Her profound empathy and commitment make her a beacon of hope for those seeking solace and transformation in their lives.

Milton Keynes UK
Ingram Content Group UK Ltd.
UKHW020129070524
442290UK00014BC/624